*A*ppreciation

*T*o:

*F*rom:

ISBN: 1 86476 403 1

Copyright © Axiom Publishing, 2006.
Unit 2, 1 Union street, Stepney, South Australia 5069

AXIOM
AUSTRALIA

www.axiompublishing.com.au

Printed in Malaysia

Appreciation

*T*he grand essentials to happiness
in this life are
Something to do,
Something to love,
And something to hope for.

essentials

remember

You have to take the good
with the bad, smile with the sad,
love what you get,
remember what you had,
always forgive, but never forget,
learn from your mistakes,
but never regret, people change,
things go wrong, just remember,
life goes on.

$\mathcal{A}$ppreciation is a wonderful thing:
It makes what is excellent in others
belong to us as well.

— Voltaire

$\mathcal{L}$ove me when I least deserve it,
because that's when I really need it.

love me

wisdom

$\mathcal{K}$indness is more important than wisdom, and the recognition of this is the beginning of wisdom.

— Theodore Isaac Rubin

Someone out there is meant to be the love of your life, your best friend, your soulmate, the one you can tell your dreams to. He'll smile at you when you tell him, but he'll never laugh at your heart. He'll brush the hair out of your eyes and send you flowers when you least expect it. He'll call you to tell you goodnight before you get into bed or just because he is thinking about you.

He'll be bursting to talk to you each morning just to hear the sound of your voice. He'll look into your eyes and tell you that you are the most beautiful girl he has ever seen and for the first time in your life... you'll believe it.

meant to be

There is a sacredness in tears.
They are not the mark of weakness,
but of power. They speak more
eloquently than ten thousand
tongues. They are messengers of
overwhelming grief...
and unspeakable love.

— Washington Irving

$\mathcal{E}$njoy the little things in life,
for one day you may look back
and realise they were the big things.

little things in life

$\mathcal{M}$ake it a habit to tell people
thank you.
To express your appreciation,
sincerely and without the
expectation of anything in return.
Truly appreciate those around you,
and you'll soon find many others
around you.
Truly appreciate life, and you'll find
that you have more of it.

— Ralph Marston

appreciate

*I*t is one of those beautiful compensations of this life that no one can sincerely try to help another without helping himself.

— Ralph Waldo Emerson

for others

What we have done for ourselves alone dies with us; what we have done for others and the world remains and is immortal.

— Albert Pike

$\mathcal{K}$indness is more than deeds.
It is an attitude, an expression,
a look, a touch.
It is anything that lifts
another person.

— C. Neil Strait

$\mathcal{L}$ife without love
is like a tree without
blossom and fruit.

— Kahlil Gibran

without love

*H*umankind has not woven
the web of life.
We are but one thread within it.
Whatever we do to the web,
we do to ourselves.
All things are bound together.
All things connect.

— Chief Seattle

never forget

As we express our gratitude, we must never forget that the highest appreciation is not to utter words, but to live by them.

— John Fitzgerald Kennedy

kindness
beauty
truth

The ideals that have lighted my
way and time after time have
give me new courage to face life
cheerfully, have been Kindness,
Beauty and Truth.

— Albert Einstein

$\mathcal{T}$rue, we love life, not because we are used to living, but because we are used to loving. There is always some madness in love, but there is also always some reason in madness

— Friedrich Nietzsche

*H*appiness needs sadness.
Success needs failure.
Benevolence needs evil.
Love needs hatred.
Victory needs defeat.
Pleasure needs pain.

The most beautiful things
in the world are not seen
nor touched.
They are felt with the heart.

— Helen Keller

*T*o the world you may be
just one person,
but to one person
you may be the world.

one person

The purpose of life is
not to be happy.
It is to be useful,
to be honourable,
to be compassionate,
to have it make some
difference that you have
lived and lived well.

— Ralph Waldo Emerson

purpose of life

value

$\mathcal{Y}$ou must experience and accept
the extremes. Because if the contrast
is lost, you lose appreciation;
and when you lose appreciation,
you lose the value of everything.

to have loved

I hold it true, whatever befall;
I feel it, when I sorrow most;
'tis better to have loved and lost
than never to have loved at all.

— Alfred, Lord Tennyson

$\mathcal{T}$he roots of all goodness
lie in the soil of appreciation
for goodness.

— The Dalai Lama

goodness

*T*wo kinds of gratitude:
The sudden kind we feel
for what we take;
the larger kind we feel
for what we give.

— Edwin Arlington Robinson

gratitude

$\mathcal{L}$et us be grateful to people who make us happy; they are the charming gardeners who make our souls blossom.

— Marcel Proust

upwards

$\mathcal{T}$hose who are lifting the world upward and onward are those who encourage more than criticise.

— Elizabeth Harrison

and onwards

special

There has never been another you. With no effort on your part you were born to be something very special and set apart. What you are going to do in appreciation of that gift is a decision only you can make.

— Dan Zadra

fundamental things

The more one does and sees and feels, the more one is able to do, and the more genuine may be one's appreciation of fundamental things like home, and love, and understanding companionship.

— Amelia Earhart

$\mathcal{B}$e content with what you have;
rejoice in the way things are.
When you realise there is nothing
lacking, the world belongs to you.

— Lao Tzu

be content

simple smile

We shall never know all the good
that a simple smile can do.

— Mother Teresa

life of a child

A hundred years from now
it will not matter what my bank
account was, the sort of house
I lived in, or the kind of car I drove,
but the world may be different
because I was important
in the life of a child...

—Forest Witcraft

light from within

$\mathcal{P}$eople are like
stained-glass windows.
They sparkle and shine
when the sun is out,
but when the darkness sets in,
their true beauty is revealed only if
there is a light from within.

— Elizabeth Kübler-Ross

*L*augh when you can,
apologise when you should,
and let go of what you can't change.
Kiss slowly, play hard,
forgive quickly, take chances,
give everything and have no regrets.
Life's too short to be anything
...but happy

Life is about who you love
and who you hurt.
It's about how you feel
about yourself.
It's about trust, happiness,
and compassion.
It's about avoiding jealousy,
overcoming ignorance
And building confidence.
It's about what you say
and what you mean.

It's about seeing people for who
they are and not for what they have.
Most of all it is choosing to use
your life.
In a way that could have never
been achieved otherwise.
These choices are what life's
about.

$\mathcal{T}$oo often we underestimate the
power of a touch, a smile,
a kind word, an honest compliment,
or the smallest act of caring,
all of which has the potential to
turn a life around.

— Leo Buscaglia

potential

$\mathcal{L}$earn as if you were going to live forever. Live as if you were going to die tomorrow.

— Mahatma Gandhi

you are not alone

$\mathcal{E}$very now and again take a good look at something not made with hands, a mountain, a star, the turn of a stream. There will come to you wisdom and patience and solace and, above all, the assurance that you are not alone in the world.

— Sidney Lovett

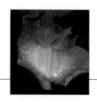

Being loved by someone
gives you strength
While loving someone deeply
gives you courage.

$\mathcal{A}$ppreciation can make a day
—even change a life.
Your willingness to put it into words
is all that is necessary.

— Margaret Cousins

*T*here is a calmness to a life lived in gratitude, a quiet joy.

— Ralph H. Blum

someone

someday

Someday you're going to meet
someone who drives you mad.
Who you're going to fight with
and laugh with and do totally
insane things for.
Someone... who turns your life
upside down.

the way I feel

Sometimes I just can't ignore
the way I feel
when I see you smile.

shown in acts

*T*hankfulness is the beginning
of gratitude. Gratitude is the
completion of thankfulness.
Thankfulness may consist
merely of words.
Gratitude is shown in acts.

— Henri Frédéric Amiel

$\mathcal{N}$ot what we SAY
about our blessings,
but HOW WE USE them,
is the true measure of our
thanksgiving.

our blessings

— W. T. Parker

What you put out comes back.
The more you sincerely appreciate life
from the heart, the more the magnetic
energy of appreciation attracts
fulfilling life experiences to you,
both personally and professionally.
Learning how to appreciate more
consistently offers many benefits
and applications.

Appreciation is an easy heart frequency to activate and it can help shift your perspectives quickly. Learning how to appreciate both pleasant and even seemingly unpleasant experiences is a key to increased fulfillment.

— Doc. Childre and Sara Paddision

be the one

I want to know what makes you cry, so I can be the one who'll always make you smile.

$\mathcal{N}$ever close your lips to those whom you have opened your heart.

— Charles Dickens

*M*aybe God put a few
bad people in your life,
so when the right one came along
you'd be thankful.

— Andrea Kiefer

the right one

$\mathcal{L}$ife doesn't have to be perfect
in order to be wonderful.

— Annette Funicello

$\mathcal{N}$o act of kindness,
no matter how small,
is ever wasted.

— Aesop

act of kindness

Love is a hidden fire,
A pleasant sore,
A delicious poison,
A delectable pain,
An agreeable torment,
A sweet and throbbing wound,
A gentle death.

love is

— Fernando de Pujas

_A_t the first kiss I felt something melt inside me that hurt in an exquisite way. All my longings, all my dreams and sweet anguish, all the secrets that slept deep within me came awake, everything was transformed and enchanted, everything made sense.

first kiss

— Herman Hesse,
Narcissus and Goldmund

together

To love is not
to look at one another,
But to look together
in the same direction.

— Antoine de Saint Exupery

When travelling the path of life, and finding love along the way, everything looks new and different. Little do you know it is the same old landscape you used to see all of the time; love has just given you new eyes.

path of life

$\mathcal{L}$ove is but the discovery
of ourselves in others,
and the delight
in the recognition.

— Alexander Smith

Don't go for the looks,
it can be quite deceiving.
Don't go for wealth,
even that fades away—
go for someone who makes
you smile because only a
smile makes a dark day
seem bright.
Hope you find that person.

only a smile